Ferrets:

A Complete Guide

By Diana Geiger

Paddy Paw Books

Ferrets: A Complete Guide

Content copyright © 2011

By Diana Geiger

Paddy Paws Books

First publishing date - August 2011

Published in the United States of America

Please visit exoticpets.bellaonline.com

Dedication

This book would not have been possible without the support of my family. My soul mate, friend, and husband George Geiger and also my daughter Erika D Hisel-Behlke.

I owe a tremendous amount of gratitude to my father Howard V Jones. He gently prodded me along to write. He would be adamant that I had talent and insisted I write a book, though he felt I was wasting my time writing about exotic pets! But Dad, I like exotic pets! Dad, I love you RIP.

The first article I wrote was about my son's tragic death. Robert V Ruth (October 11, 1979 to February 11, 1995) was always an inspiration and I miss him dearly.

Table of Contents

Chapter One: Introduction to Ferrets

Ferrets are friendly little animals related to the weasel. Though their appearances are similar, their mannerisms are not. The weasel reminds me of a dysfunctional weed eater with their sharp little teeth. Ferrets are usually quite sweet and loveable.

Ferrets have been an important part of our lives for many years, bringing a great deal of joy to our home. They are more entertaining to watch than any television show, especially right after they have had a bath. They stagger as if they are intoxicated. It seems that they can't walk; they move forward on their stomachs, roll, and then rub up against everything; trying get rid of the water.

Ferrets are every bit as intelligent as a dog or a cat, though sometimes it won't seem that way because of their silly antics, and what seems to be a lack of coordination. They can easily get carried away while playing and jump backwards and then fall on the floor. At other times their dexterity is finely tuned, moving quietly and cunningly.

The scientific name for the ferret is Mustela Furo, Mustela Putorius Furo of the order Carnivora. All this mumbo jumbo means the ferret is a carnivorous mammal of the Mustelidae family. Other members of the Mustelidae family include weasels, otters (both sea otters and river otters), minks, ermines, martins, badgers, and many others.

The ferret is the third most popular pet, third to the dog and the cat. They make a remarkable pet for the right person, though I strongly advise that you learn as much about the ferret as possible before you consider purchasing or acquiring a pet ferret. You need to spend time with an actual ferret to understand what these little animals are like. Do you have a friend with a ferret or ferrets? It is best to go into ferret ownership with experience and awareness. Also, make sure you have found a veterinarian knowledgeable about ferrets before you acquire a ferret.

Ferrets make a sensational pet because they are intelligent, loving, entertaining, and can be quite comical. Having a ferret as a pet can enrich your life considerably. Ferrets are very intuitive. They can also be quite spontaneous.

Adjectives that describe the personality of a ferret are conniving, devious, tricky, sly, and wily. But they can also be affectionate, charming, and loving. But, all in all they are all rabble-rousers!

Ferrets have a lifespan of six to ten years. They normally remain alert, active, and playful well into their "golden years." I had one ferret that was born blind and got along very well with this sensory disability. He lived to be seven years old and remained king of the mountain until he passed away.

Many people will suggest not buying just one ferret and say that a single ferret will get lonely. I have seen many people with a single ferret. As long as you spend quality time with him or her, your ferret will do just fine. I have had a single ferret only once. That was my first ferret. Soon after buying the first ferret I bought a second, then a third, until I had seven ferrets. They do love to play together. Whether you have a single ferret, or two, or a business of ferrets, it is your decision. They are a very social animal, if you choose to have a single ferret it is your responsibility to provide the play and love that they require.

They love for you to be at their level, on the floor to play. Supply your ferret or ferrets with lots of toys of different varieties, soft, hard, squeaky; they like variety.

They love to cuddle but on their terms. When they are released from their cage to play, they are ready to play right now! Ferrets may have time for a quick pet and kiss, but they are ready to go! After playtime they will begin to seek out a place to sleep. This is a good time for loving and cuddling.

Ferrets have been found to be valuable as service animals; their intuitiveness enables them to anticipate seizures and then warn about the impending seizures in children and adults. Many veterans that were injured, fighting for our country, depend on the ferret's ability to detect and warn about seizures. Children are able to enjoy a more contented, full, and joyous life because of this amazing ability. Ferrets have been a valuable aid to children with autism. Service ferrets perform an important service in nursing homes and hospitals.

Having a ferret as a pet can also have its downfalls. They don't always use the litter box. They sleep about 20 hours a day, and ferrets have a distinctive odor.

The scent glands near the anus are normally removed before you purchase a ferret. These glands release pungent oil when the ferret is scared. This is somewhat like the skunk but instead of a spray it is more like seep or ooze. There are also oil glands in their skin; much of the odor comes from these glands.

Spaying and neutering the ferret also helps with the musky smell. An unaltered male can have a very strong smell. Once neutered the male smells no worse or better than a female.

A ferret shouldn't be bathed very often. It really doesn't help with the odor. Too much bathing can actually make the odor worse. If their skin dries out from too much bathing, the oil glands will go into overtime. Keeping their bedding clean helps a lot to minimize the odor. Have several changes of bedding. When you fill their water bottle each day change their bedding.

Their excrement has a very strong odor primarily because ferret food has a strong odor. Some brands of food are worse. Though, I wouldn't use an inferior food just because it has a milder odor. Simply scoop their litter box a couple of times a day.

I buy rose scented garbage bags at the dollar store. I use the bags mostly in the winter when there is snow on the ground. Otherwise I take the soiled litter outside and mix it with the soil; away from my vegetable garden. It is good for the soil; usually my hedge roses get the treat. In the winter I scoop the litter box, place it in the rose scented bag, and tie a knot right above the litter. The next time I scoop it goes above that knot. I don't like to use any more plastic than necessary. The bag of litter goes into a tightly closed diaper bucket, or any container that seals tight. Plastic cat litter containers are good for storing bagged, used litter. A couple of times a week, someone will brave the snow and empty the litter container into the outside garbage can.

Ferrets can be destructive. They may scratch up your carpeting, your bed, or any number of other things. They may chew up your stuff.

Your house must be ferret proofed making sure there are no holes where they can get stuck or escape. You must make sure they can't get near dangerous objects, poisons, and other contaminates. They will stick their head into anything trying to fit the rest of their body through the object. Because of their pear shaped body they can get themselves firmly stuck.

Because of their curiosity and intelligence they are always investigating their surroundings. It seems like every ferret has his or her own obsession. One of my ferrets loves remote controls. If she finds one she chews the buttons off. Another one steals any metal object. After all ferret are excellent thieves. Years ago I had foam rollers for my hair; one by one they disappeared. When I was packing to move to a new house, I found a huge stash of foam hair rollers in the loft. The point being, a true ferret person loves these endearing antics, if these humorous performances don't appeal to you, you're not destined to be a ferret owner.

Ferrets like any other pet needs to be supervised around children and children supervised around ferrets or any other pet. There have been a few incidences of ferrets causing injuries to children, particularly infants. Face it, animals are animals, and don't forget to include humans into that animal category. I believe per percentage, humans have caused far more harm than pets. Humans cause injury maliciously. Pets injure by accident unless they have been hurt, frightened, or abused.

A baby or small child has a rubbery feel to their fingers and toes. A ferret doesn't know these rubbery things are fingers or toes. They feel like toys, therefore, they're going to play with them as if they are toys. A ferret doesn't give up a toy easily, often resulting in a game of tug-a-war. A ferret's mentality does not often surrender. I think you get the idea, please don't leave a baby or small child alone with a ferret.

Male ferrets are called hobs and female ferrets are called jills. Neutered male ferrets are called gibs and spayed female ferrets are called sprites. If you get a bunch of ferrets together, they are a business of ferrets. Nothing is closer to the truth; a bunch of ferrets is certainly busy. A baby ferret is called a kit, and is a bundle of joy.

Female ferrets are normally smaller than a male ferret. Females are 13 to 14 inches long (0.3302 m to 0.3556 m) males are 15-16 inches longs (0.381 m to 0.4064 m). A female will weigh approximately 0.75 to 2.5 lbs (0.340194 kg to 1.13398 kg), a male 2 to 3.5 lbs (0.907184 kg to 1.58757 kg). A neutered male is a bit smaller than a non-neutered male.

Ferrets have a wide variety of colors and patterns. One of the most common is sable. There is also a dark sable which doesn't have the light undercoat or warm brown tones that the sable has. You will also see albino ferrets. Albino is the absence of color or a pattern. The albino ferret is white with red eyes. The albino ferret shouldn't be confused with the dark eye white ferret, a white ferret with brown or black eyes.

My first ferret was champagne (a cross between a light tan and white color) my second ferret was a black and white. My third ferret was a cinnamon which has a light undercoat and reddish brown guard hairs. There is a wide variety of silver ferrets from light to dark silver with a white undercoat. The silver ferret can have black, dark, or blue eyes. All these colors, except for albinos, can have a wide range of beautiful patterns.

All ferrets have unique and individual personalities. If any of these qualities bother you, please don't acquire a ferret. If you read through this book with a silly grin on your face, you could very well be a ferret person.

As with any pet, you need to learn as much as you can before obtaining your ferret. Doing your homework first saves a tremendous amount of heartache.

Chapter 2: Housing the Ferret

Ferrets are cold and heat sensitive. Ferrets have been domesticated for thousands of years. They don't belong outdoors. Anything below 50 degrees or above 80 degrees could put the ferret's life in danger.

Humans and many other animals have the benefits of perspiring. In hot weather we perspire, the perspiration evaporates cooling the body. Air moving through the perspiration also cools the body. Ferrets don't perspire. That is why temperatures above 80 degrees can be deadly to ferrets.

Keep your ferrets out of direct sunlight. The room you house your ferrets in should have air conditioning, a window unit if you don't have central air. A fan alone won't help since the ferret doesn't perspire. If you supply wet burlap, blankets, or other materials that will absorb water, putting this in front of a fan will help. Keep a spray bottle full of cool water and mist the ferrets. Once the ferrets or blankets dry, the cooling affect will be gone. It will have to be repeated often.

If you use a fan, keep it out of the ferret's reach. That fan blade will cut off little noses, legs, or just plain kill the ferret.

Keeping a shallow bowl with a few ice cubes available on hot days will help. Tiles, like you'd use in the kitchen or bathroom, feel cool to the ferrets. Put some tiles on the floor of the ferret's cage or let the ferrets hang out in the kitchen or bathroom, with supervision. Take care that the toilet lid is closed and held down by a heavy object. Make sure they have bedding material in their temporary quarters.

You'll need to be ready if the electricity goes off during hot weather. Keep milk jugs, liter soda pop bottles, or like objects partly filled with water, and freeze them in the freezer. Make sure you have plenty. The freezer should stay cold for a day or two. Put the frozen containers in the cage or keep the ferrets in a confined space with a frozen bottle or two. Change the bottles when they melt.

Don't fill the containers all the way, when the water freezes it will expand. Wrap a towel around the frozen gallon milk jugs or stick a soda bottle inside a sock, use anything to protect their skin from the frozen container. You don't want to injure your ferrets trying to keep them safe and cool.

If the electricity goes out in the winter, especially if you live in a cold climate, you must have a means of keeping the ferrets warm. A gas, diesel, or propane generator is a lifesaver for your ferrets and your family. A generator will allow you to use devices to keep your ferrets either warm or cool.

Everyone should have a generator, not only to protect your pets but for a variety of reasons. If you have a freezer full of meat, losing it all will be a very pricy loss... Generators are worth their weight in gold! Shop around, prices vary a great deal. Make sure the generator is kept outdoors; you don't want to kill your pets with fumes or carbon monoxide. Never use a barbeque grill, gas, or charcoal inside.

I occasionally take my ferrets outside to play for short periods of time. I have taken them out with the assistance of a few other people, to briefly (a couple of minutes) play in the snow. They can tunnel through the snow very quickly. This is the reason I have other people help; you just never know where a ferret will emerge in a snow bank. I would rush them back inside and dry them. By then they would already be shaking. They love digging in the soil, playing in the leaves, sniffing fresh air. If they have had their vaccinations; short amounts of supervised outdoor playtime is beneficial to the ferret.

The best housing situation for a domesticated ferret is a large, safe, multiple level cages, inside a house. They need plenty of opportunity to play outside the cage every day. Ferrets are very active animals; the bigger the cage the better. Even then, they need plenty of time outside of the cage in a ferret proof environment. There are many hidden dangers to ferrets. Because of their determination and size just about any hole or space can be a temptation leading to potential disaster.

If there is a small space under a door, chances are a ferret can get under it. With their small heads and pear shaped bodies it doesn't seem possible, but they are able to flatten themselves to the size of a thick carpet.

Heater vents, duct work, and drier vents are all places a ferret can escape. They may not even have escape on their minds; if there is a hole a ferret will investigate it. I have had more than one ferret stuck in a tube-like object. Raising kids and ferrets together you don't always have complete control over what is strewn about.

I have often been fortunate to have the space to allow the ferrets to have their own bedroom. Even then, I would be 100% certain the bedroom had no escape routes only to find a ferret missing. Believe me when I tell you they can fit through the smallest of places. They stand at a good level to spot any hole that you may never find. Don't think they won't try the bathtub drain. They are very determined when their curiosity gets the best of them.

There are many multi-level ferret cages with ramps leading to each level. These cages are great; except for some of the cages have poor welds or areas where the wire has been attached. These connections can be fatal to toes and toe-nails. Bar spacing on a cage specifically for a ferret is usually sufficient except with kits (baby ferrets). I keep my kits in a small pet porter until I am sure the kit can't get through the bars. I also keep them separate from the adult ferrets because adults love to drag the kits. The kits aren't too thrilled about being dragged around. You also have to keep kittens and other small animals away from adult ferrets for the same reason.

I don't use an aquarium. Even with a mesh top there isn't enough circulation in a glass or plastic enclosure. There can also be a moisture buildup that can cause serious respiratory and skin infections. These are caused by funguses and bacteria leading to serious illness and even death. Glass and plastic enclosures can also get very hot.

Most multi-level ferret cages have a metal tray on the bottom of the cage. Ferrets have a tendency to dig in their litter box or food dish and scatter the contents. Their tray does help contain the contents. The tray makes cage cleaning easier as well.

Metal trays can rust. When cleaning and disinfecting the cage make sure to dry the cage. Also, keep blankets or carpet on the bottom of the cage, and change frequently. This will help keep things dry to prevent rust. Before using any bedding material, examine the blankets and carpets making sure the ferrets can't get their toenails stuck in the weave. Watch out for frayed edges so that the ferret can't get entangled and strangled. I have found that the best carpets are the old rag carpets. Rags were stitched together then crocheted into dense-tightly weaved carpets.

Use some heavy material, especially in the winter, ferrets like to be warm. Again, ferrets are very temperature sensitive. Don't let them get too hot or too cold. Use plenty of bedding. Be sure to offer light weight material as well; let them have a choice. They can make up their own beds. Don't forget to change the bedding often.

Second hand stores are great places to shop for ferrets. You can buy heavy sweatshirts for bedding material. You can cut out the sleeves of sweatshirts to make your own hammocks. You can either make tube hammocks or open hammocks. Leave some extra material on the sides and cut some strips to tie the hammocks to the sides of the cage. You could also cut strips of material and stitch it to the sleeves, using the strips to tie the hammock to the cage.

I buy baby receiving blankets for warm summer use. I put several in the cage on top of the more durable material. They can choose their own blankets and how much material they want to use to cover themselves. Tee-shirts are another example of great ferret bedding. Again, second hand stores, and your own dresser or closets, make great places to gather bedding for ferrets.

They like and need dark hiding spots. One type of hiding spot is a bed that hooks to the ceiling of the cage; an example would be tunnel beds. These types of hidey spots are essential to their mental health. Ferrets are naturally tunnel dwellers; they like to feel safe and to sleep in dark places.

Ferrets have sensitive feet. The wire cages are rough on these sensitive feet. Cover the wire with heavy material.

I like the food dishes that connect to the cage walls. These work out great because you can control the height, position, and it keeps the ferret from tipping over the dish. I currently have a dish for each ferret. They share a cage and have learned where their own dishes are located. These dishes are only used for vitamin oil. We let the ferrets out each morning to play. When they go back to their cage they have their goodies waiting for them. By goodies I mean their vitamin oil. This is primarily the only treat they are allowed. I have bought ferret meat treats but the ferrets weren't too impressed with them. They love their vitamin oil. I use or have used **8 in 1 FerreTone Skin and Coat Supplement, Marshall Furo-Vite, Furo-Tone**, and **Furo-Vite Paste**. The paste is great to help a ferret put on weight if it has been under the weather. Once opened, use it up; it will spoil. Keep oil in a cool place or refrigerate.

When the ferrets are put back in their cage after playtime we would put them in front of their own dish. Over time they learned which dish was theirs we can just set them in the cage, and they will trot up to their own dishes.

Make sure the litter box is a corner litter box made for ferrets and connects to the cage with clips. The clips are necessary; otherwise the ferret will push the litter box out of the corner. The corner ferret litter boxes have a high back because ferrets have a tendency to hike up their rear ends to eliminate. They also like to do their business in corners; this is the reason for the high back, corner litter box.

You will need a couple of extra corner litter boxes when they are playing outside of the cage. Also make sure the food dishes, water bottles, and vitamin dishes are at the opposite end of the cage or at least above the litter box, so that the food and water doesn't get contaminated.

Clumping litter isn't very healthy for ferrets. Ferrets like to dig and dredge their noses through the litter. Clumping litter is very dusty. When they bulldoze with their noses through clumping litter, it can cause respiratory problems. The stirred up dust isn't good for animals or for people to breath. Remember, if you can smell an odor, a remnant, however miniscule, of what caused the odor it is entering your nose and mouth. Clay litter is also too dusty.

I like the recycled paper pellet litter. Never use pine or cedar shavings; the noxious oils in pine and cedar shavings are deadly to ferrets and all animals. Pine and cedar shavings have killed many ferrets, rats, and mice. You get the picture. Please don't use these shavings in animal cages.

Buy good quality water bottles and make sure you have more than one. The gravity water bottles that hang on the side of the cage have a tendency to fail. I always use two water bottles just in case one should stop working. Using dishes for water is messy and unsanitary.

I still prefer food dishes that attach to the side of the cage. But, I do use one heavy crock food dish. They love to dig in their food. With ferret food being rather pricy, and too much was being wasted. I cut out the bottom of a plastic litter jug or gallon milk jug, and placed the food bowl inside of this container. Now the food falls inside the second dish, rather than scattered all over the cage floor.

This perimeter dish holding the food dish also acts as a safety feature. Ferrets like to push things around. Using a cage with multiple layers, there are ramps so that the ferret can get to each level. My ferrets like to push the food dish down the ramps, which would be a disaster if it should hit another ferret. The cut-down litter jug keeps the dish in a stationary location.

Chapter Three: Nutritional Needs

Ferrets are carnivorous. They have a short digestive tract. The digestive tract is much too short to digest the nutrients in plants. The ferret's digestive system does not include a caecum (also spelled cecum) which is needed to digest vegetables, fruits, and grains (plant foods). The caecum is a cavity at the beginning of the large intestine. Herbivores have a large caecum; the caecum contains bacteria that assist with the breakdown of plant food (cellulose) through an enzymatic action. Since ferrets don't have this caecum, the ferret is an obligate carnivore.

Because of the short digestive tract, food goes through quickly. They must have high levels of animal protein and fat in their diets. Ferrets also have fast metabolisms and must have food available to them all the time. They can starve to death in a relatively short period of time.

There are several decent ferret diets available.

Ultimate 8 and 1 has 45% protein; the first two ingredients are chicken and chicken meal and 16% fat. **Totally Ferret** lists chicken by-product meal as the number one ingredient and rice flour as number two. **Zupreem** 42% protein lists chicken meal as the first ingredient and sweet potatoes as number two. **Marshall Premium** has 38% protein, 18 % fat and list the first two ingredients as chicken by-products (organs only, including chicken liver) and herring meal. There are several more ferret foods on the market. Check the protein (make sure it is an animal based protein), fat, and also the main ingredients. If the main ingredient is not meat, keep looking.

Since none of the commercial ferret foods is ideal, you can supplement their diet with cooked, not raw, meat; these include chicken, organ meats, or lamb. You can also include cooked egg. Yes, wild ferrets eat their meat uncooked, but these uncooked prairie dogs or rabbits have not been contaminated by human hands. Wild animals also consume parasites with their uncooked wild diet. We don't want our domestic pets to have parasites.

Even if you do supplement with cooked meat, you should give them a vitamin supplement. Ferrets need vitamin supplements every day. As I wrote earlier I have used **8 in 1 FerreTone Skin and Coat Supplement, Marshall Furo-Vite, Furo-Tone, and Furo-Vite Paste**. All are good supplements. I use them as a treat because ferrets seem to love the taste of the vitamins. Most importantly, these vitamins contain taurine. Taurine is an amino acid and it is essential for ferrets.

Marshall Uncle Jim's Original Duk Soup Mix is good for older ferrets, ferrets with digestive disorders or a ferret that seems to be going downhill.

When I have a sick ferret I use warm water, soak ferret food, and give spoons of this soaked water to the ferret to lap. I give them as much as they will take. I give it to them often. It helps keep them hydrated and they will receive some nutrients. Better yet, add some of the Duk Soup Mix. Give them some vitamin supplement oil. If they won't take it from a spoon put it on your fingers so that the ferret can lick it off. Put it on their paw if that doesn't work. Rub tiny bits on their lips. Make sure to keep it away from their noses you don't want them to inhale it and aspirate. Don't force it on them; that too can make them aspirate.

They must eat meat not corn, wheat, rice, and other additives found in dog food and cat food. Ferrets can never be fed dog food or cat food. They must have a high quality ferret food. In an absolute pinch they can have a high quality kitten food for a very short period of time, for a couple of days while you get ferret food. Changing diets is very hard on ferrets, don't run out of food. We are talking, short-term, real emergencies when you feed kitten food.

If for some reason you must change ferret diets, do so gradually, very gradually. Ferrets have sensitive stomachs. Perhaps you have acquired a ferret from someone else and don't feel the food the ferret had been eating is nutritious, or a worse calamity, the manufacturer that created the food went out of business. Change to the new food gradually. Add a little at a time to the old food until they are eventually changed over to the new diet. How gradual the change is may depend on how much of the old food is left.

If you use treats use a meat based treat. Fruit based treats are not good for ferrets. Peanut butter is vegetable protein; again the ferret cannot digest vegetable proteins. I have tried some of the meat based treats. I started my ferrets out as purists and none of the treats has impressed them. They would rather have their vitamin oil as a treat.

Ferrets like vitamin oil so much you can use it to help with some chores such as trimming nails. Put some oil on the opposite paw you are clipping. While they lick the oil clip their nails. You can also clip nails while they sleep. They sleep very soundly!

Ferrets, humans, and a wide variety of animals must have some sunlight every day. They need the sunlight for the formation of vitamin D. It is important for the absorption of calcium. Specifically D3 is necessary and it is available in most ferret foods and ferret vitamins. It is not a water soluble vitamin, so the amounts found in the food and vitamins are not quite adequate. Some exposure to indirect sunlight has many added health benefits.

Since there are so few things ferrets can safely eat, stick with their regular food and vitamins. There is a long list of things they can't have. If I cited this long list there would be approximately only five things remaining, high quality ferret food, cooked meat (not deli), ferret vitamins, ferret meat treats, and filtered water.

Ferrets should always have access to fresh filtered water. Your gravity water bottles should be cleaned and the water changed daily. The water bottles should be sanitized weekly. If you use bleach, rinse the bottle well.

Some people recommend bottled water instead of tap water. These people don't realize, and this is a fact, that bottled water is tap water, nothing more, often less.

A friend of mine owns a store in California. Mostly it is a fruit/vegetable stand, a huge fruit/vegetable stand. He also carries dried fruit, nuts, and a combination of herbs, spices, and so forth. He is on a busy corner of two major highways. This store is located in San Joaquin valley and it gets very hot. He thought it would be a good idea to carry bottled water.

He attended a symposium by a major distributor of bottled water that is owned by one of the huge cola product companies. Come to find out, bottled water is nothing more than tap water, whatever is available at the plant where bottled water is filled. He opted not to sell bottled water.

Then think about the bottled water sitting in plastic containers for long periods of time, usually in very hot warehouses. All the chemicals that make up a plastic bottle leach into the water. So, not only do you have just tap water, but contaminated tap water; it is more contaminated, since tap water is contaminated to begin with.

Bottled water, by federal regulation, only need be as good as tap water, not better than tap water. "Companies that market bottled water as being safer than tap water are defrauding the American public," Food and Drug Administration (FDA). *Bottled water companies make about 22 billion every year.*

Neither tap water nor bottled water is good for you, pets, or exotic pets. Always use a filter, a good filter to filter your water.

Always use filtered water, never bottled water, or tap water. Store filtered water in glass.

Chapter Four: Ferret Fun

The more intelligent the animal, the more complicated the play; and this certainly includes ferrets. Ferrets are also very social animals and need plenty of quality time with their human family, even if they have other ferret friends to play with.

Ferrets burn a tremendous amount of energy when they play. They have two speeds, fast forward and stop. They sleep about 20 hours a day. When they sleep they can appear dead to the world, or at least to you. Their heart rate slows and their breathing can be virtually unnoticeable. More than once I thought I had found a dead ferret in the cage. They will even slump like a wet rag if picked up. I have broken into tears only to have a ferret suddenly looking at me, "What's the wrong Mom?" If they're not sleeping, they are ready to play.

Right after they wake up they need their litter box, right now! After using the litter box, they are lined up at their cage door, ready to be picked up. We basically have the same routine every day. I assist them with their prison break – you would think so, by the way they rattle their cage; then I take them into the bedroom. I drop them on the Select Comfort (air bed) where my schizophrenic Ragdoll cat sleeps; they attack the cat, and the cat swats them. Then they start searching for toys. Or, they may start burrowing in the blankets instigating a game of cave. The game cave means I get teeth in my fingers.

If the ferret is on the floor jumping up and down and tugging on your pants leg, it means they want you on the floor. If they are acting spastic and making chirping noises, that means they are content, happy, and having fun.

Ferrets love tunnels. You can buy tunnels at any pet store or you can make them out of most anything. Just make sure the tunnel is big enough so that the ferret doesn't get stuck or hurt. They love carrying around small stuffed animals. They enjoy pushing or pulling balls. It usually doesn't make sense to buy the most expensive of anything. Buy them the expensive six dollar ball, and they will ignore it. Then they will play with the old scuffed up plastic golf ball. Go figure! Buy a ten dollar stuffed animal and they play with the old stuffed animal that looks like the only decent thing to do would be to bury it. Boxes and bags are a blast. Anything that rustles or crackles is fun. Investigating is a favorite ferret pastime. Just changing a room around a little bit will keep them entertained for a while.

I found a toy at Cracker Barrel; it was more than I would normally pay for a toy. It is battery operated. This toy has a little motor inside a ball and the ball has a fuzzy tail. It moves about and abruptly turns different directions; it was a blast putting it into a paper bag. I just knew the ferrets would love it. They were curious at first. Especially with the object moved and rustled the paper bag. After a short investigation they happily went looking for their battered stuffed animals and homemade toys. The cat sniffed it, when it turned toward her she ran under the bed; brave kitty.

Knotted old socks make wonderful toys for most people's ferrets but not mine. One of my ferrets likes to wash socks.

Each ferret has a favorite "thing"; one loves rubber and plastic objects, such as remote controls. One ferret likes metal objects and will steal any metal object she can carry with her. One has a fixation on socks and washing socks. This was the craziest thing, anytime someone would remove a sock and forget to put it in the dirty clothes hamper, she would find it;

place it in the cat's water dish, take it out and run around with it. If she found a way into the dresser I would have a mound of wet socks.

My ferret Missy recently passed away. Years ago, the same day I bought her; I also bought her a stuffed frog. The frog would wiggle and jump when a string was pulled. She loved that frog. She carried it everywhere with her. She was very possessive of her toys. If I got her toys out of her hiding spots she would promptly haul each one back to where it belonged. As she got older she would only haul back her favorites. Then it was only her frog she would return to the stash. Toward the end if her life, I would hold her and her little frog. She looked happy when she had her frog.

Favorite games are hiding and go seek. You hide they seek, or they hide, and you can't find them. You continue seeking until they can't maintain self-control any longer, then you have a spastic, chirping ferret pulling at your pants leg. Another fun game is chase. Get down on the floor with them and crawl after them. A game of Tug of War is always great fun. An old knotted up sock works as well as anything else. They will do their cute backward hop and chirp in delight.

After a while, I will leave them to play on their own and go back to my home office to work. A little later I'd go check in to check on them and they are nowhere to be seen. All have gone to find cozy places to sleep. This is when you have to be extra cautious. They don't have the ability to pick safe sleeping spots. They could be asleep under something that dropped on the floor. They could be under the bedding on the bed. Or under the mound of pillows the cat sleeps on. (This makes me think of the Princess and the Pea.) Just be careful where you sit or walk. Considering I have had several groups of ferrets several times in my lifetime, things can still happen. Just the other day the phone rang. I walked into the bedroom. Walked close to the bed, the comforter had one end lying on the floor. I felt something warm next to my foot. I had come that close to stepping on a ferret. It just takes an instance to have your mind on something else to spell disaster.

When ferrets are awake they enjoy playing, and being with you. They love for you to be at floor level with them.

Since I do the majority of my reading lying on the bed because of my spine injuries, after the ferrets are done playing they will often climb up on my stomach to be petted. There they will fall asleep.

Chapter Five: Ferret Training

Wait, or is that people training? Training ferrets is really no different than training a dog or even a whale. The key to training any animal is positive reinforcement, patience, consistency, and never using physical punishment, a stern NO, will do the trick. Ferrets are sweet little critters and are quite willing to please.

For example, if you see a ferret using the litter box praise him or her vocally and give your ferret a tasty treat. Again, vitamin oil is an excellent treat. If you catch the ferret backing into a corner to do their duty, pick the ferret up, vocalize a firm no, and then place the ferret in the litter box. If the ferret then uses the litter box use positive reinforcement, vocally praise the ferret, and give the ferret a treat.

It is a good idea to start your new kit or new ferret out in a confined space. Put a little box in the corner. Ferrets will always use some sort of corner, backing into the corner with their little rear ends hiked up to eliminate. As the ferret becomes proficient in the small space, add a little more space. When their space is expanded it may be necessary to have an extra litter box in another corner.

One litter box training mistake many people make is cleaning out the litter box completely. If you always remove all the feces and urine the ferret will think it is doing something wrong, and shouldn't eliminate in the litter box. Always save a bit of feces and a small clump of urine soaked litter to place in the clean litter box.

Another reason ferrets don't use their litter box is because some people are just plain too lazy to scoop out the litter box daily. I wouldn't want to stand in a litter box with waste material squishing between my toes either. I wouldn't want to stand in a stinky litter box and a ferret has a better sense of smell than we do. It only takes a minute to clean out a small litter box.

Ferrets have a tendency to forget to use the litter box on occasion. If you find an area they have chosen to use as a toilet put a litter box in that place. Perhaps there is a litter box they have stopped using. Put that litter box in their chosen corner.

Sometimes they will get in a big hurry. They will back up to their litter box, stop short of it, squat with their little behinds in the air, and miss the litter box entirely. I bought plastic carpet protectors and placed a good sized square under the litter box with a portion sticking out.

Ferrets will most likely never be perfect when it comes to the litter box. This is something you need to consider before purchasing or acquiring a ferret.

Ferrets nip each other in play, it's a natural behavior, but it is an unwanted behavior when they are playing with their human family. If they nip, immediately stop playing and voice a firm no. Then walk away. They are very social and friendly, it won't take long for them to realize nipping causes the end of playtime and that nipping is an unaccepted behavior.

You never want to hit a ferret or flick a ferret on the nose or face. This will cause the ferret to fear you. You would also be reinforcing a bad behavior, the biting would continue. It would no longer be a nip but a painful bite.

If a ferret is injured it may bite, and bite hard. Years ago one of our ferrets got his foot caught in the wire cage. We tried to help the ferret get his foot out. The ferret was in a great deal of pain, trying to extract the foot caused more pain and I received a nasty bite. This is not a behavior to punish, it was a natural reaction.

One of the first things you will want to teach your ferret is to come when called. This is for your ferret's safety. If you start with more than one ferret you will need to train individually. Otherwise, you will be teaching all the ferrets to come when called. When the ferret comes up to you use his or her name. Soon the ferret will recognize his name. When the ferret comes to you when you call it, reinforce the behavior with praise, love, and a speck of vitamin oil. It doesn't hurt to shake the vitamin bottle when you call the ferret's name; the more association the better.

You can also use ferret meat snacks. Most come in a foil-like bag. Rattle the bag to associate the noise with the treat. So, when you call the ferret's name, you are rattling the treat bag or shaking the vitamin bottle. When he or she comes to you, you give pats, a treat and vocalize in a happy voice what a good, use the ferret's name. Eventually, the ferret will be thrilled to please you. Pats, hugs, kisses, and vocalization will be enough positive reinforcement.

Training, using positive reinforcement works on almost any animal. If you use punishment, your ferret won't trust you or want to please you, and will in fact fear you.

Chapter Six: Health/Medical Issues

I have been pretty lucky. Most of my ferrets have lived to old age. Rarely have they been sick. What I call luck probably had little to do with luck. It is keeping the animals healthy. Keeping the animals healthy is feeding them healthy food, fresh clean filtered water changed daily, more often in warmer months. We keep up with their vaccinations.

Prevention

Something I know as fact, keeping their surroundings sanitary keeps the veterinarian away.

Their food dishes and water bottles are cleaned and sanitized daily. Their litter box is changed and sanitized daily. The cage is cleaned daily and sanitized weekly. Their bedding is changed daily. That is more for our benefit than their benefit. The odor from the oil glands in their skin is kept down by changing out their bedding every day. We wash their bedding in hot water. We keep our pet's contact with other people to a bare minimum.

However, ferrets metabolize very quickly, they are small, and they can get ill very quickly. Ferrets can also show endurance, rarely complain, and can hide their illnesses quite effectively. Many animals will hide illness, showing weakness is an invitation to predators. If your ferret shows any signs of illness get your ferret to a veterinarian immediately.

If your ferret should show signs of an illness, for example adrenal disease, it can be treated and it isn't as expensive as you might imagine. Another thing you should be aware of, the cost of veterinarian care can differ a great deal from veterinarian to veterinarian. Shop around!

When you consider purchasing or acquiring a pet, make sure you are able to be financially responsible for the animal. You can't feed the cheapest food and expect your animal to thrive. You have to keep up to date on vaccinations and check-ups. Pets need to be spayed and neutered. Pets can and do become ill, make sure you have a fund set aside for illnesses and accidents.

Stress decreases the immune system. Your ferrets will be more prone to illness if kept in a stressful environment. Also, keeping your ferret or ferrets caged all the time is stressful. If they have no human contact they will wither, become ill, and eventually die. They are highly social animals and need time with you and time outside of their cage.

You simply cannot give your ferrets junk food, non-meat items, or treats with sugar. The ferret is not designed to digest these foods. It will lead to illness and death!

Vaccinations

Vaccinations should only be given to healthy animals. If your ferret is ill contact your veterinarian for advice.

Ferrets are highly susceptible to canine distemper and it is always 100% fatal. The American Ferret Association (AFA) recommends a series of PUREVAX® FERRET DISTEMPER shots for a ferret kit. After the series the ferret should receive an annual distemper booster.

The recommended ages for ferret kits to have these vaccinations, is eight, eleven, and fourteen weeks of age, with a yearly booster shot given one year after the last distemper vaccination.

Adult ferrets that haven't had the canine distemper vaccination should be vaccinated, contact your veterinarian for canine distemper vaccination information. The will also need the three injections and a yearly booster.

The AFA also states that all ferrets are required to have a rabies vaccination IMRAB®3. Should the ferret happen to bite someone, and has had a rabies vaccination the ferret will go through a quarantine period instead of the ferret being put to death, and then tested. In the United States there has never been a known case of rabies being passed from ferret to humans.

The recommended rabies vaccination age is twelve weeks of age followed with a yearly booster shot.

Ferrets should only receive single agent, vaccines (monovalent). Canine distemper shots are a combination vaccine (multivalent) and should not be given to ferrets.

Some veterinarians use Galaxy® D, though it is a single agent vaccination it has not been approved for the use on ferrets, its use would be considered off label. The company that produces Galaxy® D does not offer any guarantee when medications are used off label.

Ferret Disorders

Cancer

Cancer of several varieties seems to be afflicting ferrets more frequently. Cancers that affect ferrets also metastasize quickly. Early diagnoses are essential. Once symptoms present themselves the cancer is already likely in a late stage.

What can be done? Have a complete physical with blood work at least once a year. If your ferret demonstrates the slightest of symptoms, have a veterinarian do a complete examination including blood work. Ferrets are hardy and don't get sick very often, however; when they do get sick, it often seems to be related to one of the cancers that affects ferrets.

Why is cancer so prevalent in ferrets? It is the most common cause of death and illness in ferrets. A large percentage of ferrets will have cancers at some point in their lives. Many ferrets I have seen, that have had one form of cancer or another, came from breeders that spayed and neutered extremely early. Another factor is a poor diet. As I stated before they must have a quality, high protein, healthy fat diet, they are obligate carnivores. You are not saving yourself a penny by giving them cheap cat food; in fact feeding cheap foods will cost you a fortune in veterinarian expenses. Never feed junk food. Never feed sugary sweet treats.

Breeders that know little about genetics will inbreed, an additional potential factor causing ferrets to be prone to cancer. Another theory is a virus causing the cancer problems. Hopefully, someone will get to the root of the causes of the following cancers.

Insulinoma (cancer of the pancreas) can be verified with blood work. Many veterinarians will want to start out with ultra sound. Unless they are planning to perform surgery I'd start with blood tests. Ultrasound is a non-invasive way to discover the type of tumor and location of tumor before surgery.

Excision of the tumor may save your ferret, though this type of cancer does metastasize quickly and has a high rate of reoccurrence.

Ferrets can be made more comfortable with prednisone (a synthetic steroid hormone anti-inflammatory drug,) and diazoxide. Surgery is often necessary. The ferret will need regular blood work to check on low blood sugar levels and perhaps insulin levels. Giving 1/8 a teaspoon of brewer's yeast can help regulate blood sugar.

Insulinoma can occur at any age but most common at 4 to 6 years old. The onset of insulinoma can be very sudden and severe or very gradual. It can also occur concurrently with lymphoma and adrenal disease.

Watch for sluggishness, weakness, hind leg weakness, coordination problems, weight loss (though the ferret may still have a normal appetite). Drooling, pawing at the mouth, foaming at the mouth are all symptoms of an upset stomach which goes along with insulinoma. Ferrets may have seizures due to low blood sugar. These seizures can be fatal.

If your ferret has a seizure, do not force liquid or food into its mouth. Take a little corn syrup or honey and run a little on the ferret's gums and inner lips. Use a Q-tip to avoid being bitten while the ferret is seizing.

If your ferret has any of these symptoms contact a veterinarian immediately.

Lymphoma/ Lymphosarcoma are the most common cancer found in young ferrets usually up to two years of age.

Lymphosarcoma can also progress rapidly in young ferrets. Symptoms include vomiting, diarrhea (can be black and tarry-like stools), and dehydration, taking strength and energy from the ferret, and making the ferret very thin. Once the thymus becomes involved, the ferret will cough and can have difficulty breathing.

You may notice the lymph glands swollen behind the back legs, under its arms, and or around the neck.

With all cancers it is essential to contact a veterinarian immediately.

Lymphosarcoma can be misdiagnosed, if you suspect Lymphosarcoma insist that it be ruled out. Make sure you are dealing with a veterinarian with plenty of ferret and cancer experience. If the ferret has a biopsy make sure the pathologist also has ferret experience.

Lymphosarcoma can also rear its ugly head in older ferrets. This form is a disease of the peripheral nodes. As the disease progresses it will spread to the kidney, liver, lungs, and spleen

Adrenal Disease (adrenal gland tumor) is another very common cancer in ferrets. In fact, around 40% of ferrets will end up with adrenal disease. Some people say that 50% to 80% of ferrets born in the United States will be affected with Adrenal Disease.

Suspected reasons include early spaying and neutering, too much light (ferrets are naturally tunnel dwellers), poor diet, and in-breeding.

Adrenal Disease is where one or both of the Adrenal Glands have lesions or tumors. The majority of the time only the left

Adrenal Gland is involved. Adrenal Glands are located in close proximity to the kidneys, and to the front of the kidneys.

The Adrenal Glands produce hormones such as estrogen and testosterone. When the Adrenal Glands are not working properly it contributes to the symptoms of Adrenal Disease.

One of the main symptoms of Adrenal Disease is hair loss most commonly beginning at the tip of the tail or lower parts of the body. They will continue to lose hair until often becoming completely bald. Other symptoms include, weight loss, tiredness, swollen vulva on the female and enlarged prostate on the male. The enlarged prostate will cause the male ferret to have difficulty urinating. The skin can thin considerably taking on an orange tint. The muscles will waste and the ferret will become weak.

The veterinarian will diagnose Adrenal Disease using physical signs, blood work, and x-rays. Ultra-sound may be used.

Treatment usually requires surgery, some medications can be used, but it is not the treatment of choice. Several hormonal therapies are being researched. Contact a veterinarian immediately if you suspect your ferret has Adrenal Disease. Use an experienced ferret veterinarian.

Infectious Diseases

The average heart beat of the ferret is 33 to 36 breaths per minute. The normal temperature of a ferret is 101.9 (taken rectally) 99 degrees to 100 degrees by ear. You can use a rectal or an ear thermometer. When you buy a new thermometer rectal or ear; do so when the ferret is healthy. Take a baseline temperature for each ferret. Be very careful inserting either thermometer, you can cause injury. Record the baseline temperature.

Get use to how warm your ferret feels to your cheeks. When the ferret has a fever you'll feel it.

If the ferret registers a fever take the ferret to a veterinarian for a checkup and blood work.

Ferrets with viruses or bacterial infections can waste rapidly; they are small and metabolize quickly. It is important to keep your ferret hydrated. You can use Pedialyte. Pedialyte is an oral rehydration liquid designed to restore lost fluids and electrolytes. It may be necessary for your veterinarian to rehydrate your ferret by using subcutaneous fluids. This is where a specially formulated liquid is injected under the skin.

Don't give your ferrets aspirin unless prescribed by a veterinarian. Aspirin use is for extreme cases only and only under the supervision of a veterinarian. Aspirin toxicity happens quickly and frequently with ferrets.

Colds and Influenza

Ferret can catch the flu and colds from humans. They can catch it from other ferrets and other animals. They were/are susceptible to the HIN1.Thank goodness the H1N1 didn't go rampant.

Keep people that are ill away from your ferrets. If you are sick have someone else in the family care for your ferret. If that isn't an option, wear a facemask and wash before handling the ferrets or anything that comes in contact with the ferrets.

If your ferret shows symptoms of sneezing, runny nose, watery eyes, coughing, loss of appetite keep the ferret comfortable and hydrated. Separate the sick ferret from your other ferrets and animals.

Take your ferret to a veterinarian if any of these things happen: your ferret doesn't show improvement in a few days, or if the ferret is having trouble breathing, if you hear chest wheezing, if the ferret has completely lost its appetite, or if the ferret has discolored discharge.

Epizootic Catarrhal Enteritis (ECE)

Epizootic Catarrhal Enteritis (ECE) is a highly contagious virus, it is also known as the green slime disease because one of the symptoms is green slimy diarrhea. Other symptoms include loss of appetite, weight loss, grainy stool, vomiting, and lethargy. The ferret can remain contagious for up to a year or longer. Though there is no cure, it is rarely fatal in a young healthy ferret and the symptoms usually last just a few days. The symptoms can last for quite some time in an older ferret or a ferret with additional illnesses, from a few weeks to a few months. It can be fatal in older or sickly ferrets. The virus attacks the digestive systems and can leave permanent damage. Keep the ferret hydrated.

Since a ferret can succumb quickly from disease, especially a ferret that is vomiting and/ or has diarrhea, you should always contact a veterinarian.

ECE can fool you, the initial symptoms can disappear in a few days, and you are fooled into thinking your ferret is better, while the disease progresses to the digestive tract where it can do severe damage.

I have soaked high quality ferret foods in warm water and have spoon fed the liquid frequently throughout the day. Use this with Marshall Uncle Jim's Original Duk Soup Mix. I use these and Pedialyte with each feeding. Feed every hour to keep the ferret hydrated. This has certainly saved more than one of my rescue ferrets.

Canine distemper

Though this has been discussed, it is highly contagious and always fatal. Get your ferret vaccinated. You will find more on canine distemper toward the beginning of this chapter.

Non-Infectious Health Issues

Blockages

Blockages can be a life-threatening problem. During the spring and the fall they will lick their fur and can get hairballs. They also like to investigate about anything which includes sampling; this can also cause a blockage.

You can prevent hairballs by frequently brushing your ferret or ferrets with a soft brush. Blockages from foreign objects - you can attempt to prevent these blockages by limiting access to objects with rubber, foam rubber, Styrofoam, rubber bands, fillers in quilts, or pillows, string, balloons, and some cloth materials. Keep an eye on their bedding. If they have chewed it, take it away. For some reason, those type of material intrigue them. Use something else.

Blockages usually require surgery. It is essential to get your ferret to a veterinarian immediately should the ferret show signs of a blockage.

Symptoms include, weakness, little or no stool, scrawny stools, straining when attempting to have a bowel movement, blood in the stool, vomiting, diarrhea, little appetite or no appetite at all. If your ferret is displaying these symptoms contact a veterinarian immediately.

Poisons

Poisons are abundant in households and ferrets seem to be able to find them. They can fit into tiny openings, love to chew on plants, or get into rodent or insect poisons. If a pill is dropped on the floor the ferret may investigate the pill and lick it. It doesn't take much to harm a ferret. If you know what your ferret has gotten into, bring it to the veterinarian with you. If it isn't portable write down the ingredients or name.

Here are some poison control centers, few are free anymore.

ASPCA Ani-Med 1(888)721-9100

ASPCA Animal Poison Control Center 1(888)426-4435

National Animal Poison Control Center 1(800)548-2423

Kansas State University Veterinary Teaching Hospital (Free) 1(785)532-5679

Pet Lover's Helpline 1(900)776-0007

Tuft University School of Veterinary Medicine 1(508)839-5395

Aplastic Anemia

A female ferret should be spayed. Aplastic Anemia is a common cause of death. Take your ferret to a veterinarian and have her spayed as a preventative measure!

Once a female goes into heat, she stays in heat making her estrogen levels critically high, which is toxic to bone marrow. There are only three ways to get a ferret out of heat; the first is to mate her, a very bad idea. Read the chapter on breeding. Mate her to a male ferret that has had a vasectomy, another idea that usually doesn't work. It can cause pseudo-pregnancies or she will just soon go back into heat. Then you're back in the same sinking ship. The third option still isn't a good option. About the only option you have until you can get the female spayed is take the female ferret to the veterinarian for a "jill jab" a hormone injection that will bring her out of season.

Symptoms of Aplastic Anemia are severe anemia, pale gums, lethargy, hair loss, and a swollen vulva. Get that female spayed, or it won't be long before there will be a complete loss of red blood cells.

Anal Gland Impaction

If the scent glands haven't been removed, ferrets can suffer from anal gland impaction. There are two little glands, one on each side of the anus. These glands can become impacted or blocked. An infection can set in if the glands do become blocked. Or, an infection can cause the blockage.

The ferret may demonstrate symptoms such as scooting his or her rear across the floor. Sometimes these glands can rupture leading to serious infections. Take your ferret to a veterinarian. It is a good idea to have these glands removed.

Congestive Heart Failure or Cardiomyopathy

Congestive Heart Failure or Cardiomyopathy is pretty much just like a human being gets; the heart becomes weak and can't do its job, pump blood. The blood will fill in around the lungs and the heart. Symptoms can be treated to make the ferret more comfortable, but the disease will eventually run its course.

Symptoms include difficulty breathing, tiredness, weakness, and a consistent cough. Get your ferret to a veterinarian if it should demonstrate these symptoms. The ferret can be treated with diuretics. Keep the ferret cool and calm, stress makes matters worse.

Internal and External Parasites

Internal and external parasites would include fleas, mites, and worms.

Fleas

If your ferret gets fleas, the fleas can quickly make the ferret anemic causing the ferret's immune system to quit protecting the ferret. The ferret could rapidly become ill or die from the anemia.

Ferrets can also have allergic reactions to fleas.

Ferrets are also sensitive to flea powders and shampoos. I would get a veterinarians recommendation. However, to control fleas it is necessary to use a complete programs not just treat the animal. Most ferrets get fleas from dogs and cats that go outdoors.

Complete programs include the lawn, the carpet, furniture, cages, bedding, and all animals in the household.

One of the safest flea and tick treatments and perhaps one of the oldest is **Pyrethrin** (generally safe) is extracted from the flowers chrysanthemum plants; the stuff is very effective on bugs. It is generally considered safe on kits and even kittens. Be sure to check with your veterinarian first. Do not confuse Pyrethroids with Pyrethrin it is not safe to use on cats and is more toxic. Pyrethroids are similar to pyrethrins but are manufactured chemicals toxic to cats and some other mammals.

Remember when treating for external parasites to remove your pet insects, and arachnids and other small animals to someone else's house!

First vacuum everything, carpet, furniture, and crevices. Remove the bag from the vacuum and seal it up in a plastic bag. Throw it away. Remove your animals from the house and spray the carpets and crevices in your homes. Use a Pyrethrin product recommended by a veterinarian.

Clean the ferret's cage. Wash all toys and bedding in hot water. Dry in a hot dryer. Don't forget the litter box. Dump it, wash it, sanitize it, and set it in the hot sun. You have to control the eggs and larvae, not just the adult fleas.

Flea eggs take anywhere from a couple of days a couple of weeks to hatch into larvae. Since there are over 2000 species of fleas there is a variation on incubation. Though, for ferrets, the most likely flea suspect is the cat flea, but not always.

Larvae can take a week to a couple hundred of days munching on dead skin and other organic materials until they cocoon much a like a butterfly. They can remain in this state for as long as a year or more or as short a time as a few days. They can sit in that cocoon until they know there is something to eat.

Let's say a house has been vacant for several months. The house is finally rented out. The cocooned fleas hear or feel the new occupants and they hatch for their new food supply. Adult fleas can live a long time.

That is why I call flea control a program. You have to be consistent and vigilant. Do the above routine weekly. Even after there is no more sign of fleas repeat every few months. Be extra attentive in the spring and summer.

I use Advantage on my animals, the kind where you put the little drop on the back of the animal's neck. Keep your animals separate until the spot is dry. They will lick each other's wet Advantage spots. Some people prefer Frontline. Do get a veterinarians recommendation for flea and tick products.

The same routine works for ticks. Ticks carry all sorts of disease. To name a couple, Rocky Mountain spotted fever and Lyme's disease. Ask your veterinarian for a topical tick-control product such as Advantage or Frontline. Some products are way too toxic for ferrets and two of these would be Defend and BioSpot

Mites

Mites are another external parasite that affects dogs, cats, and ferrets. A symptom is a dark, nasty, often stinky, waxy substance in the ferret's ears. The ferret may shake its head and scratch at its ears.

Since it does affect other pets you will have to treat all pets at the same time. Again, it will take persistence and more than one treatment to get rid of the mites. The mites can cause serious ear infections so it is important to treat the animals right away. Check with your veterinarian for a miticide safe for your ferrets.

Mosquitoes

Mosquitoes are a concern if you keep your ferrets outside. If you don't live in a perfect climate ferrets don't belong outside, except for short supervised play periods. Mosquitoes are blood sucking disease carrying insects that will bite your pets. Only the female mosquito sucks blood. The male mosquito actually drinks nectar.

Ferrets can get heartworm from mosquitoes! One single mosquito can give a ferret heartworm; one heartworm can kill a ferret. Ferrets rarely show symptoms of heartworm until it's too late. Keep your ferrets away from mosquitoes.

Talk to your veterinarian about mosquito prevention. I use Heartgard pills for cats. I split the pill for a five pound cat in half and give half a pill to each ferret every month.

If you must take your ferret outside, buy a generous amount of mosquito netting. Secure the netting around the entire enclosure of the ferrets play area or cage. Keep the ferrets inside the house during the worst mosquito biting time, and that would be from dusk to dawn. You can also reduce the risk of mosquitoes to yourself, family, and pets by dumping out any standing water.

Internal Parasites

Roundworms

Roundworms are a rare problem in ferrets. If you have any concerns discuss it with a veterinarian. The veterinarian can assess the situation.

Cryptosporidium Parvum

Make sure you cook the meat you feed your ferrets; Cryptosporidium parvum is common in ferret kits. There are no published reports of Cryptosporidium parvum being passed to humans, though I suppose it is possible. Healthy kits usually can kick the parasite in a short time. Adult ferrets are rarely affected.

If your ferret should display any symptoms, it is always better to be safe than sorry, get the ferret to a veterinarian for a checkup.

Coccidia

Symptoms are weight loss and bloody stools. Coccidia can be diagnosed using fecal testing and is treatable with medication.

Giardia Lamblia

This is rarely seen in ferrets and is treatable with a liquid medication prescribed by veterinarians. Giardia Lamblia is diagnosed using fecal testing.

Chapter Seven: Breeding Ferrets

Breeding ferrets is not for the timid. That is why I personally feel that I should leave it up to the experts. For many reasons breeding ferrets is not for the faint of heart. Especially, if you don't like gross odors or dreadful looking ferrets. Breeding is very stressful and often deadly for the jill and hob. The kits often suffer a high mortality rate.

Breeding ferrets can be expensive unless you have access to a free veterinarian, breeding ferrets isn't financially feasible. If you are breeding ferrets just because the kits are cute, it is irresponsible to breed ferrets.

An unneutered hob will go into rut usually about thirty days before the jill goes into heat. Then, the jill usually isn't receptive to the hob for approximately fifteen days after she goes into heat. If you attempt to put the jill in with the hob any earlier, the jill will be uninterested in the hob. That is going to make the hob mad and he could injure and kill the jill.

There is nothing romantic about a ferret's sex life, at least from my perspective. Who knows how the ferrets feel about the whole situation?

Let's discuss the Neanderthal hob that is holding an imagined club. The hob in rut puts off a very offensive odor that comes from the scent glands and his urine. The scent is made up of an oil based material which he uses to mark his territory. He scents his territory to attract females.

The oil is downright vile. The oil is spread via his underbelly. After the oily scent coats the underbelly he begins to spread the scent. In a short period of time the male is covered with this oil which makes him stink. I suppose he probably thinks my favorite cologne stinks as bad as I think he stinks!

The hob's personality becomes as offensive as his odor. The hob becomes very aggressive and certainly is no longer pet-like. After his body is engorged with hormones, they really never return to their previous sweet personalities. Though, once an unneutered hob reaches sexual maturity, they really don't make the best of pets. Of course, there are exceptions to the rule.

You will see physical evidence when the jill comes into heat. The vulva swells up and this is the sign that she is in heat. Jills do go into heat more than once a year (polyestrous).

When the hob is in rut and the jill has been in heat for approximately two weeks, the jill should be put in with the hob. The physical act appears quite violent. The male will grab the nape of the female's neck and drag her as he moves backwards across the cage. The jill will appear to be, or is in, considerable pain. She will likely scream. This is the way of the ferret, and the only way ovulation can take place. The jill may allow herself to go completely limp as if she is being treated like an old dishrag.

After competition, the jill and hob will be stuck together for quite some time; they are literally locked together. Like many mammals the hob has a baculum a bone found in the penis. In different mammals the baculum will be a different shape. The hob has a J-shaped baculum. Never try to separate the jill and hob; this would result in severe injury.

After the animals separate and before you return the jill to her cage inspect her carefully for any injuries. Be especially prudent looking for puncture wounds. Treat the wounds. If the wounds are serious, take the animal to a veterinarian.

The vulva should return to its normal appearance after intercourse in 7 to fourteen days. If it doesn't return to normal the pregnancy didn't take place.

The gestation period for a ferret pregnancy is approximately forty-two days. Many complications can occur before and during delivery. Make sure you have access to a competent veterinarian if problems should take place.

The pregnant jill will need a diet rich in protein and calories. A small amount of cooked organ meats would be beneficial too. Small amounts of cooked chicken livers will help with the needed iron. Get the very best ferret food that can be found and even then, supplement it! She will soon be lactating and nursing her young. That takes a great deal of protein, fat, and calories as well!

As birth draws near she will want to make a nest. Provide torn up paper (no colored newsprint or colored paper) and never use pine or cedar shavings.

She will give birth to a bunch of tiny, blind, deaf, and naked kits. They will be so small a newborn kit can fit inside a teaspoon. The average size of a litter of kits is seven to eight; there can be more or less. Sometimes there can be many more. The jill only has seven serviceable nipples. If she has a huge litter it becomes your responsibility, an exhausting responsibility, to raise the kits she is unable to care for herself.

Leave the jill and kits alone for a week. She will only leave her kits for a short period of time, to eat, use the litter box, grab a drink of water, and back to the kits. Seriously, they will kill and eat their young if you bother them! After a week you can sneak a peek by diverting her attention; a very quick peek.

Ferret kits will spend all their time growing, so they will suckle and sleep. As they get a little older, they will begin to learn what a ferret needs to know through play. Don't be surprised if they are playing one moment and fall asleep the next. They can fall asleep quite rapidly and in whatever position they were in last.

The kits' eyes should open at about twenty days old. You should be able to get a good idea what color the ferrets are going to be. Most ferrets are shipped from the breeders to pet stores from seven to eight weeks old.

Kits are carried and dragged by their mother as she holds them with her mouth by the scruff of the neck. She will drag them backwards; this is a common way for ferrets to move things around including her kits. As the kits get a little older, around four weeks they develop this look in their eye, "Ah mom leave me ALONE!"

After the kits become mobile the mother ferret has her hands full. She hauls them back to bed, as she goes after the next kit, out comes the one she put to bed. As the kits grow older they have spurts of energy but will still sleep the majority of the time.

Begin weaning at around six weeks of age. Don't skimp on the quality of food. These babies need high quality, ferret food, and to be fed often. The mother will continue to need extra food, only returning to her normal diet after the babies are gone. I "free range" my ferrets, meaning they always have food available no matter where they are in the house. I keep the cat's food away from them; at least I do the best I can.

The miracle of birth is a beautiful experience; however, it does have to be approached with caution. What are your motives for breeding your ferrets? If you end up with a litter of twelve will you be able to find all twelve of the kits loving forever homes? If you think you're going to make a fortune, remember the kits have to have their scent glands removed, first shots, and spayed or neutered. You may also incur many veterinarian expenses you hadn't foreseen.

Another thing to take into consideration is that every time I go to Petco to check out the kits, I discover that many of their ferrets haven't sold and have grown past their "cute baby age."

Pet ferrets should be spayed or neutered; all of the hormonal/in-season stuff is stressful on the ferrets. The jills are induced ovulators, meaning they must wait for the male's stimulation for ovulation to take place. If the jill remains in heat for an extended period of time, she could die of estrogen toxicity, Aplastic Anemia, or a variety of other health problems.

I highly recommend leaving breeding to the experts.

Chapter Eight: Your Ferret's Arrival; Kits and Adults

If you are acquiring a kit to add to your ferret family, be sure to quarantine the new arrival before putting the kits in with the other ferrets. This goes for any new ferret added to the mix. You don't want to expose your ferrets to a disease or bug.

I had the strangest thing happen. I had a kit enter my exotic pet rescue center! I quarantined it from the other ferrets; however, my Ragdoll cat ended up with an ear full of ear mites. My cats never go outside. This particular cat never leaves the bedroom, not for years. The new ferret showed no signs of ear mites. It is still a mystery.

When acquiring a new kit or adult ferret, make sure the kit's eyes are clear. Look in their ears for signs of mites. You will see a dark crusty substance. Make sure there is no discharge from the nose or eyes. Healthy ferrets are lively. They should have long silky, smooth, shiny hair. Ferrets may be asleep, but once awake it doesn't take long for a baby ferret to begin playing.

Ferrets can be bought in many pet stores and pet warehouses such as Petco. If bought from a reliable source, instead of a backyard breeder, they will be spayed, neutered, and have their scent glands removed.

Ferrets can be adopted from local shelters; in fact I strongly encourage ferret adoption. Many people get ferrets and end up surrendering them to a shelter or local ferret rescue for whatever reason; the primary reason is because they didn't do their homework before acquiring the ferret. This irritates me to no end. Ferrets don't always hit their mark in the litter box. Spayed and neutered ferrets still have a bit of an odor. The ferret food has a strong odor, therefore making the feces a bit strong smelling. All pets have their downfalls, I strongly suggest you find out what those downfalls are before you purchase or adopt a ferret.

The mother's milk is very rich with protein and fat. When a ferret is weaned they must have a meat diet, real meat like ground chicken or turkey is great. If you must use a dry ferret kibble get the best. Do not feed cat food; it has only 30-33% protein. It's full of corn and other plant matter that a ferret cannot digest. They also need healthy fat, vitamin E, taurine, amino acids, and a variety of other required nutrients. The food they eat must be high protein, highly digestible, and have healthy fat. A poor diet will starve the ferret to death.

Because of the ferret's short digestive tract the food stays in the digestive tract only a short period of time. The adult ferret needs to be fed about every three hours, a kit much more often. They must eat frequently.

Don't skimp on the quality of food. These babies need high quality, ferret food, and to be fed often. I "free range" my ferrets, meaning they always have food available, no matter where they are in the house. All kits should have food available at all times.

Watch the size and shape of the food you give your ferret. Rounded foods with a hole in the center can get stuck on a tooth, and this can cause serious pain and difficulty for the ferret.

They also become accustomed to their food, and can have digestive disturbances if their food is abruptly changed. If you must change their food, do so gradually. Use the food they are used to, then add small amount of the new food. Gradually increase the new food until you get them changed over completely.

Kits and adult ferrets should have fresh, filtered water available at all times.

The ferret usually develops their full personality around eight weeks of age. At this age you can usually assess what an individual ferret will be like. I am not saying if you find an abused ferret at a rescue, that ferret's disposition will never change. It may take some time, a lot of love, but that ferret's personality will eventually be what is was meant to be.

When you bring home a small kit, keep them separate from the adult ferrets until the kits are big enough to fend for themselves. Gradually introduce the young kits to the adults. Ferrets just love to drag young kits around. Adult ferrets love to drag any baby pet around. Kitten, puppy, it doesn't matter, if they ferret is able, it will drag a baby; if it isn't able, it will still try!

Chapter Nine: Lost Ferrets

Few things are more heart breaking than losing a beloved pet. From the day you obtain your ferret or even before you have a ferret, begin making preparations should your ferret become lost. Don't worry, if you already have a ferret we will cover all bases on finding your lost ferret.

It isn't hard to lose a ferret. They can slip out of the smallest of openings. Do your absolute best to locate these openings before acquiring a ferret or letting it have run of the house. Heater vents and duct work, dryer ducts leading to the outside of the house, or holes around plumbing are all ways a ferret can find himself or herself outside of the house. Go over the house with a fine-tooth comb. Ferrets have a curious nature, and it is that curiosity that gets them into a great deal of trouble.

An open door would trigger that curiosity. During nice weather you may have a great deal of traffic going in and out of the house. A curious ferret could easily slip through a door without anyone noticing.

If your ferret is missing, call your family together and divide up the necessary responsibilities to find the lost ferret. Get your close friends involved. Make sure one person has the duty of looking through the entire house for the lost ferret. As all ferret owners are aware, a ferret can fall asleep anywhere at any time.

One of the first places to look is inside the freezer and refrigerator. If your kids were after a Popsicle or soft drink, a ferret could have slipped inside the appliance, and it won't live long if it did. Look inside the mattress covers, under or behind dressers, under any soft thing that dropped to the floor. Look inside the laundry hampers, under the pile of laundry by the washer, look inside dresser drawers. Look everywhere.

First of all, identification is important. Always have a current picture. Start your ferret out with a safe harness with an ID tag. Have your ferret equipped with a microchip. Microchips aren't just for dogs and cats!

Pay attention and memorize every little detail about your ferret. Does he or she have a dark little spot on the inside of the leg? Write down all the details and put it in a file with your ferret's important papers. These little details could help identify your ferret; it could also save your life!

There are some unprincipled people in the world. Don't give out too much information on any posters or advertisements. Someone may call to lure you into his or her clutches and harm you, or pretend to be the ferret's owner and use the information you provided to claim the ferret.

Other important preparations, besides identification, are getting the ferret used to a noise, such as a squeaky toy. In fact, when you find a toy that makes a noise that the ferret really likes, make sure you buy more than one. Put one in your lost ferret kit. It would be an awful time not to be able to find the favorite toy, or find that the noise box broke! One of my ferret's favorite squeaky toys is a plushy skunk that squeaks when squeezed. They usually prefer plushy over hard rubber squeaky toys.

Have a whistle, like the ones teachers use in school yards. Don't blow it too hard, you don't want to injure your ferret's ears. But associate the whistle blowing once a day, to you – use a treat. If the ferret hears the whistle, it knows you are near and will probably come to you. Sounds and associations could bring your dear pet back to you! Your ferret is frightened; this association and sound is a comfort, and the ferret will probably see it as safety.

Another important preparation is always keeping an extra blanket in the cage with the ferret or ferrets. It will have their scent and they will be used to it. Make sure you have a pet carrier, and make sure the ferret or ferrets are use to the carrier. If you have a single ferret you can take the cage outside. If you have more than one ferret, use the pet carrier. Place the extra blanket with their scent inside the carrier. In addition, place something in the cage or carrier that has your scent on it.

Place the ferret's cage or pet carrier near the exit, if you know where the ferret exited. Otherwise, put it near the house in a protected area. Check back often, the little ferret could curl up in the blanket exhausted, but then wake up and continue outside investigations

If you know where the ferret had exited the house immediately grab the squeaky toy and start making noise. Blow the whistle. If you don't get an immediate response figure the ferret has worn itself out and could be asleep somewhere. Go out every half hour, squeak the squeaky toy, and blow the whistle.

Ferrets are inclined to stay close to shrubs, bushes, the house, and garage, anything offering them some protection. Watch open areas for a scampering ferret, heading from one secluded area to another.

In the meantime, make up some lost ferret posters. Be sure to put your phone number and your cell phone number. Put these posters up everywhere. Be sure to check on legalities of placing posters. Ask all store owners if you may put a poster on their board or in their window. Most will be quite decent about it.

Communicating with the store owners will also make them aware of your missing ferret. They may hear of a found ferret!

Keep in mind that many people may have no idea what a ferret is. Nor do they know the variety of colors a ferret might be, so if you use the description sable they may not have a clue what sable is. They may not know the term guard hairs. So with your description add a more general description; brown with dark brown mask on face. You get the idea.

Phone any ferret rescues, ferret associations, city pounds, animal shelters, and all veterinarians informing them of your lost ferret. At that time ask if you can hang a lost ferret poster in their public areas. Inform the veterinarians if the ferret has a microchip.

Make sure you go to every single one of your neighbors and advise them that you have lost your ferret. Give them a poster with a picture. A close friend of mine lost her ferret. She lived in a fairly remote area so her closest neighbors were a fair distance away. Come to find out, the neighbor's teenage daughter had seen the ferret. We lived in an area with 10,000 plus mammals, so she probably had no idea what she had seen. Nor did she know that her neighbor had a pet ferret. Word of the lost ferret did finally get to her and that is how we found the ferret. The ferret was scratched up, bitten; we immediately took her to a veterinarian to treat the puncture wounds.

If it is cold outside remember ferrets don't do well at all in temperature extremes. Provide a warm, cozy space near where they escaped (use the scented blanket). Get an extension cord and put a heating pad on low. Remember that heating pads for human use have an automatic shut off every two hours. Turn it off and then back on before the end of the two hours. Open the garage door and provide another warm cozy spot. Check these spots you have provided frequently. Don't just look, feel for lumps! There could be a ferret under the blanket and it just looks flat with a small crease.

I mention the following story because the experience gave me a lot of insight in finding lost ferrets. I had a house up in Northern Minnesota. I had lived in California. I had two criteria when I searched for house. It had to be on a body of water. River, lake, or ocean, it didn't matter. I also wanted to be adjacent to federal or state forest. I had always loved Minnesota, so it was among my preferred states. I ended up buying a house, sight unseen, in the middle of the Chippewa National Forest, on a bluff overlooking a lake. It even had a boat house; what else could a person ask for? We packed up and moved across the nation.

It ended up being an old summer cabin full of very old personal belongings including a wringer washer. (I got a lot of use out of that old thing). It wasn't insulated! In fact, you could see light between the boards. To top that off, it was the middle of winter. To make a long story short, the ferrets could always find a way to the crawl space under the house. However, they couldn't get out of the crawl space. So I took one of their blankets, opened the access door, put the blanket under the house next to the access door. When they went missing, I'd just stick my arm through the access door, feel for warm lumps, pulled the ferrets out, and put them back in the house. I always called those blankets my ferret catchers. Blankets will almost always work!

Place advertisements in the newspaper. If you have an advertisement paper, for example The Penny Saver, place advertisements there as well. Often newspapers will allow free lost pet advertisements.

If you belong to an organization or church with a phone tree, see if you can make use of it. Use your internet social pages; get the word out!

Since every single ferret has its own personality, think about your ferret and its likes and dislikes. You might come up with the perfect idea that returns your ferret back to your arms.

Chapter Ten: Ferret Dangers

Some dangers are usually pretty obvious; some of these dangers may not occur to us at all. No matter, ferrets are curious, and much of our day to day living spaces are not safe for our ferrets.

Who would think that a ferret would climb into a vacuum cleaner and go to sleep? It's time to vacuum the carpet and the ferret could be killed. My personal way of making sure my ferrets are always safe is keeping them caged and letting them out daily for playtime. It may be several times a day, but it is always during a time when someone is there to supervise them.

At one time, many years ago, my first batch of ferrets was always allowed to run free. During that period of time we lost ferrets to stupid accidents. One was Halloween night. When the kids got home, we went through the candy, to look for suspicious items. We then put the candy up out of reach. We went to bed; however, one of our kids decided they needed a piece of candy. They had been to several Halloween parties, went trick or treating, were tired, and left the candy bag on the floor. We found a dead ferret in the morning; he had choked on a hard piece of candy.

The second accident also could have been avoided. The only time one of our ferrets decided to climb up inside a recliner was the same time one of the kids plopped themselves into the recliner. The ferret was instantly killed. We felt awful.

I quickly changed from the person that felt animals should run free, to keeping them caged until it was time for supervised play.

Open toilets make me cringe. Jacuzzis and hot tubs make me ill; any open area of water is a place a ferret can drown. Yes, ferrets are excellent swimmers, but if they can't climb out, they will grow exhausted and drown.

Rocking chairs, fold-out couches, sofa sleepers, recliners are all places a ferret may investigate, or accidently happen to be inside or underneath. All are items that can and will kill the ferret.

I had a total of twenty-one ferrets over the years; none of them ever touched an electrical cord. Then one day my laptop wouldn't start up. I did all the usual problem-solving techniques, and then looked at the electrical cord; it had been chewed completely through. Thankfully, we keep everything unplugged due to the number of electrical storms and electrical surges, even though we have surge protectors. It just takes one time!

Dishwashers, refrigerators and other appliances, again ferrets are inquisitive and love to investigate. All pose serious threats to our ferrets.

Cleaning agents can also kill ferrets. Something that appears as unthreatening as pine cleaners can kill a ferret. You mop the floor, the ferret walks across the floor getting the cleanser on their feet. They lick their feet. The stuff is highly poisonous! So are many other cleansers. It doesn't take much to kill an animal as small as a ferret.

Poisonous plants are another danger to your ferrets. Ferrets love to dig; they can't resist a pot of dirt. They may chew the plant, or just grab a leaf because it may have potential as a toy.

Some people use child-proof gates thinking it will contain the ferrets in one area. I haven't seen one yet where the bar spacing is close enough to keep a ferret from pushing its way through. I have placed acrylic sheets on both sides of the gates. As long as you don't leave them a place to climb between the gate and the wall it usually works.

Pipes are a danger to your ferret. They love to climb in holes. They can climb inside the pipe and become stuck or lost.

There are many hidden and unhidden dangers in a house. You may never see these dangers. But an animal that is low to the ground with a curious nature will find these dangers!

The best advice I can give is keep you ferrets caged except during supervised playtimes!

Something I often think about, especially since I had been a new journalist is fires and caged pets. Have a sign on doors to your house stating you have caged pets. All too often these animals will die of smoke inhalation or burn to death.

I did have a rescue skunk that came from previous owners. All these people's skunks had been in a fire. The skunks had been caged. All the skunks died except for the one I adopted. How that little skunk survived, I will never know. Please place signs or decals on your doors or windows near the door. The ASPCA does have a free pet safety package that has a window decal that informs rescue personal that there are pets inside the home. Some fire departments have the decals available as do some veterinarians. Be sure to inquire about "Save my Pet Stickers." I have rarely seen decals specifically for caged animals, only pets, dogs, or cats.

Chapter Eleven: Conclusion

Adding a pet to your household is not a decision to be taken lightly. Give it considerable thought. For some people ferrets make an outstanding pet. For other people, they will find their odor offensive, destructiveness intolerable, their everyday needs excessively extreme. It is better to know now than after you have acquired a ferret.

No two people are the same, nor do we have the same likes and dislikes. No two animals are the same. You cannot compare different pets by describing them as catlike or doglike. Ferrets are unlike any other animal. I have witnessed the diverse and unique personalities of my ferrets.

If you have read this book and have a big grin on your face, while imagining ferret antics, you could be a ferret person. Go on to the next step and find a friend or a way to get to know a ferret up close and personal.

If you are not destined to have a ferret, I seriously doubt if you are still reading this book. If you are still reading and have lingering doubts please examine those doubts carefully.

If you have an infant or small children be aware of potential dangers of ferrets hurting children or children hurting ferrets. Scrutinize these possibilities. Would you be able to supervise all interactions between the children and the ferret? Would the ferret be caged when you are not available to supervise? Would small toddlers and children have unsupervised access to the ferret cage? My concern is not ferrets and small children; it is any animal and small children.

The first time I saw a ferret I knew immediately a ferret would be part of my future. Sure enough, my first ferret tugged at my heartstrings, and stole my heartstrings all at the same time. They have given our family a tremendous amount of joy. They are also great little thieves as cunning as they come!

If you have decided to acquire a ferret I hope the ferret brings you all the happiness my ferrets have brought our family.

Please visit exoticpets.bellaonline.com here you will find a huge amount of free, high-quality information on Exotic Pets!

14106857R00043

Made in the USA
Lexington, KY
08 March 2012